Getting Re
for School

MARGARET BASHAM

Dedication

This book is dedicated to the memory of
Miss Nellie Robinson, headteacher,
Mountfield Infants' School,
Newcastle upon Tyne,
1956–1974

LONGMAN GROUP UK LIMITED
Longman House
Burnt Mill, Harlow, Essex CM20 2JE, England
and Associated Companies throughout the World.

First published 1982
New Edition 1988

Photoset in Linotype Syntax

Printed in Great Britain
by Scotprint, Musselburgh

Contents

Acknowledgements

I should like to express my sincere thanks to:

- The staff of Chopwell Infants' and Nursery School.
- The children whose illustrations appear in the book, and their parents who have allowed me to use their children's work.
- Gateshead Education Authority for appointing me to my first headship at Chopwell Infants' School and thereby giving me the opportunity to put my ideas into practice.
- Mr. John Rennie, of the Coventry Community Education Project. My book was inspired by a talk he gave over three years ago.

The author and publishers are grateful to the following for permission to reproduce photographs: Henry Grant, page 32 above; Terry Williams, page 22 above.

Photographs on pages 9, 19, 30, 37, 43, 53, 56 and 60 are by George Clark and those on pages 15, 23, 34, 36, 38, 40 and 51 by Peter Lake.

The illustrations are by Edward McLachlan and Martin Salisbury.

Introduction

Dear Parents,

This book has been written for both mothers *and* fathers and I think it important you should know why it has been written.

Twenty years ago I took my oldest boy to school for the first time. I had visited the school beforehand to find out the starting date. I was given this, told the time when I must arrive and, also where I might buy the school uniform. He wasn't being enrolled for Eton, by the way – just the State School round the corner, which had a school uniform, which was compulsory. I was then shown the door. Of course there must have been exceptions, but I believe this headmaster was typical of many headmasters at that time. I was treated as just another parent with another child – to be got rid of as quickly as possible so that he might get on with his job. I was certainly not welcomed into 'his' school in the way, for instance, I would have welcomed him into my home. His whole manner was discourteous and forbidding. Moreover, he seemed not the slightest bit interested in that third person by my side – my son and his future pupil – nor did he realise that I was eager for his advice about how I should help prepare my child for school. Did I dare ask, considering the way I'd been greeted and so quickly shown the door? No!

So I carried on doing what I could, not out of any certainty that it was correct but more by following my instincts. I suppose I was more concerned about that first day at school than I was about anything else; it is such an obviously big step in the life of any child (or parent, for that matter). Having qualified as a nurse before I was married, I had seen how so many children went through untold misery when suddenly separated from their parents – all the more so if they were completely unprepared for the separation. Similarly, though it was school he was going to, not hospital, I could put myself in my child's place and understand the misery he might feel if I didn't prepare him. We had to pass the school on our way to the shops so I used the opportunity to stop and talk to him about how grown up he was, for this would soon be his school. I told him how exciting it would be to make new friends, and to do new exciting things which he couldn't do at home . . . and so on.

Then the first day dawned. I arrived with my son (I was to go through the same performance a year later with my second son) at the correct time, with him dressed correctly, and I stood in a long line with all the other mothers and their children. When I think back, it was a remarkably well behaved line of obedient mums and children who 'knew their place'. Out of forty or more I knew only two or three, and we smiled nervously at one another. My child gripped my hand tightly, refusing to smile at anyone. My turn came and I was asked four questions:

1 Name of child
2 Date of birth
3 Home address
4 Father's occupation.

No sooner had I answered the last question than Lindsay was whisked out of sight by a complete stranger (who was still a stranger when she whisked Graham out of sight a year later).

It would shorten the story a little if I could now say, 'and they were damaged for life!' In fact, both boys settled down with almost no trouble, unlike many of their classmates. Lindsay's anxiety when he came home from school, after his first day, was that he *still* hadn't learned to read (a

My headmistress

(by Kerry, 7 yrs 5 months)

common grumble!). Graham could never run home fast enough from school to get on with what life was really all about, that is, to play! What they actually did in school was a complete mystery. They were most reluctant to tell me how they filled their hours and, of course, feeling unwelcome, I never dared return to the school to find out either what was happening or if I could help. All that seemed to be required of me was that I should feed, clothe, and generally groom them for the five days a week when they were the **property of the school**.

Thank goodness, it's *highly* unlikely that you, or your child, will experience anything like this.

After your first visit to your child's future school, you can be certain of additional assistance from the headteacher. It is in everyone's best interests that *you* should be given help but, above all, it is important for the sake of your child.

I wonder if you, along with many other parents, might make the mistake of thinking that your child's education begins the day he starts school? In fact, it begins at home and from the first moment you make contact with your child – and I *mean* from birth. Really, *you* are his first teachers and, given help, you can be the *best* teachers he'll ever have. The years at home with you are the years when he learns more (and more quickly) than at any other time in his life. If you know what to do, not just by instinct, but through having sought advice and then carrying it out, you'll be good teachers and your child will be fortunate indeed. He'll then have the chance to make the most of the expert attention of his teachers in the infants' school.

The rest of this book is designed to enable you to help your child in a number of ways. The first chapter deals with how you can best help him at home; the second, with whether or not you can choose your child's future school and, if so, how; the third, with the next stage, including registration and the practical things you

should be thinking of before he starts school; the fourth, with the night before and the first day at school, and the fifth, with school itself.

Throughout this book I refer to your child as *he*, simply for convenience. Everything applies equally to boys and girls. I also refer to your child's first teacher as *she*. This is also for convenience, although the vast majority of 'reception class' teachers are, in fact, women.

Now read on . . .!
With all good wishes,
Sincerely,

Margaret L. Basham.

Margaret L. Basham
Headteacher
Chopwell Infants' and Nursery School
Tyne & Wear

helping Your child at home

abc

Talk, talk and more talk!

Talk to your child as much as possible and, what is just as important, *listen* to what *he* has got to say to *you*. Talking to your child means including and engaging him in conversation by exchanging ideas and views, and by both answering and asking questions. The more you converse with your child, the more thoughtful he will become, and, moreover, the better you will get to know him. Never talk down to him or use 'baby' words such as 'puff-puff', 'bow-wow', 'moo-cow'. . .

He might have difficulty in pronouncing some words, but he'll learn to pronounce them accurately if *you* speak clearly. Help him with slight impediments but don't worry about them. You should be very concerned, however, if no one except the immediate family can understand a word he says. You should ask for advice from your doctor. Your child might need the expert help of a speech therapist who would also advise you as to the extra help you can give at home. Please don't wait till your child starts school before seeking help or he will have lost the chance to begin school on an equal footing with those friends who *can* speak clearly.

Never ignore or brush aside your child's questions. Answer them as simply, clearly, carefully and truthfully as you can, and don't be afraid to introduce new words. He can never have too many words on 'the tip of his tongue', **but**, before he can make sense of them and use them, he must have heard you use them in a way which makes sense to him. Your child is curious and eager to learn, and you should be doing all you can to *develop* his curiosity. There will be many times when his questions confound you, yet you must give him an answer. **Resist** the temptation to say, 'Oh, I don't know', or 'I've not got the time to tell you', or 'Oh, I'm tired of you and all your questions – go away'.

Usually simple, clear answers will satisfy

your child but you should be more pleased than displeased if the simple answer isn't enough, and he's probing more deeply. What should you do if you find you *cannot* explain further? Tell him that you don't know (or that you find his question difficult to answer), show an interest in the problem he has posed, and let him know that there are ways of finding out. Visit the library with your child and explain your problem; ask friends, or your doctor, or the health visitor, or any local expert – the plumber, the milkman, the shopkeeper, the joiner, the refuse-collector, etc. Don't be afraid to enquire – you'll find most people pleased to help provided you ask at a convenient moment. Additionally, try to work out in advance how you would answer complex questions such as:

'What's air?'

'Where did I come from?'

'Who is God?'

'What's Heaven like?'

'Where does electricity come from? How does it work?'

Just as you should be prepared to answer your child's questions simply and thoughtfully, you should be asking him questions which will compel *him* to think. For instance, instead of saying, 'I'm going to do the washing today' (knowing it's a good drying day), ask – 'Do you think this is a good day for us to do the washing?' Give him a clue by looking outside, indicating the need to observe conditions. If he seems to think it would be a good day, ask him why today is better than yesterday or why it might not be just as well to wait until tomorrow. When you've discussed this and have made your decision, let him help you hang out the wet washing and then bring it in when dry (having discussed the effects of wind and/or sun). There'll be some articles which you'll want brought in before they're completely dry – discuss this through question and answer. He will have learned so much more by discussing something which you take for granted, but which is unexplored territory to him. Let him see for

himself that clothes *don't* dry if they're hung out on the line on a damp day, or a cold day, or a wet day, or a cold, still day, even if you hang out only one article to prove the point.

Sarah has 'hundreds and thousands' of questions to ask her parents when she helps them in the garden. (Her illustration opposite indicates that the family are ready for gardening, though her parents may not realise how well prepared *they* should be for *Sarah's* questions!).

She'll want her questions answered, **but** will be just as pleased to answer those questions her parents put to her. You can avoid being besieged by thousands of questions by matching question for question, i.e. answer your child's question and follow it with a question of your own. Help your child to focus on *one* topic and discuss *this*, otherwise you'll become impatient and before long will be saying all those things you ought not to be saying, such as: 'I knew I shouldn't have brought you along'; or 'Get lost'.

Your tone of voice and your facial expression are very, very important – in fact, as important as the words you use. You can be sure your child will remember the harshness of your voice and your cross expression, even though he may not have understood every word spoken. Don't be altogether surprised, by the way, when you hear your child imitating you. He may not know the meaning of the words, but he's quite capable of repeating them using all the appropriate tones of voice, facial expressions, and gestures. If you don't like what you hear and see, scold yourself, not him, for you taught him to be a good imitator from the moment you first implored him to respond to your smile.

You have heard it said, I'm sure, that conversation is a dying art. Many things have been blamed for this: T.V.; Radio I; pop music; syphoned music in pubs, restaurants, and supermarkets; noise in industry; working mothers; the breakdown of family life; the stress of modern living;

We've got the tools for the job and while we're in the garden I've got hundreds and thousands of questions to ask.

by Sarah, 5 yrs 10 mths.

and so on. Isn't it all too easy to blame anyone or anything so long as it isn't **you**?

Conversation is a skill – it does *not* 'come naturally' – and your child has to learn the skill at home, with you. He'll learn how to converse by being included in family conversations and discussions – about holidays, trips, shopping, where to go on a wet day, what to do which would make a change from the usual routine, why one alternative is better than another, and so on. By involving your child in this way you will not only be helping *him* but also helping to revive the art of conversation.

Never give your child the impression that he's being 'grilled'. **You** don't like being 'grilled', nor would you be pleased if your questions were ignored or half-answered, or if you were excluded from a conversation. His frustration will be more

acute than any you're likely to experience, for he's only got you to turn to for help. If *you* don't help him, he'll stop asking, lose interest, give up, and subsequently find school very difficult.

Conversation is *central*, not only to reading and writing, but to every aspect of your child's learning, so **Talk, talk, and more talk** which means *Discuss, discuss, discuss.*

Television

Don't leave him to watch television on his own. You should be there to see if the programme is suitable *and* so that you can discuss the items during and after the programme. I can understand the temptation, once in a while, to place your

13

child in front of the set and use it as a 'child-minder' whilst you have a breather in another room or finish peeling the potatoes in peace, but to do this habitually is *wrong*. When my sons were young there were very few programmes for them (they belong to the 'Andy Pandy' and 'Muffin the Mule' generation) but I recollect the shared pleasure they gave us. These days, however, you are almost spoilt for choice and have four channels which give an excellent service. There are:

1 Programmes which are designed to stimulate your child's interest in a wide variety of topics (e.g. 'Blue Peter' and 'Seeing and Doing');
2 Programmes which are specifically designed to entertain *and* educate the pre-school child (e.g. 'You and Me' and 'See-Saw');
3 Children's television on BBC 1 which offers a variety of interest and usually begins with a story, pictures and songs;
4 Story time, which might not be suited to the pre-school child on every occasion but it's worth watching out for those that are. There is a good story-teller, some

visual stimulation and your child has got to listen;
5 'Rainbow', 'Just 4 Fun' etc. provide general interest;
6 If you have a video 'Watch with Mother' is an excellent tape. Just as young children love to hear the same story over and over again, so they will want to 'Watch with Mother' over and over again.

Broadcasts such as the above are most carefully produced by experts who understand the needs of young children. In some cases, these experts assist yourselves and teachers by writing pamphlets which explain the aims of the programmes and give ideas both for preparation and follow-up. Teachers use these pamphlets – *so should you*! Considering their value, the cost is small – from 15p to £1.35. Write to your local I.T.V. Publications Department, or to B.B.C. Publications, Schools Orders Section, 144–152 Bermondsey Street, London SE1 3TH.

It's important that you should *continue* to take an interest in the television programmes your child watches once he's started school, by the way – they provide you with an excellent link with school, *and* give you the opportunity to reinforce and extend his class teacher's work.

Some parents, believe it or not, deliberately decide *not* to invest in a television set because, they feel, it comes between them and their children. They'd rather entertain, help and teach their children *their* way. If you're not as brave as they are, you ought at least to think rather more carefully about the television programmes your child watches.

You'll share all the fun of the circus and of cartoons, of course, but the programmes which offer more than straightforward entertainment are the ones you should be looking out for and encouraging him to watch in preference to others. Sometimes this might mean you have to deprive yourselves of the adult 'adventure' film when a nature film, for instance, is being

shown on another channel at the same time. Ask yourselves which of the two programmes has more to offer to your child, remembering you've got plenty of time to view adult programmes when he's gone to bed.

Look at any programme through your child's eyes and try to imagine the impression it is making on him with his more limited understanding. You'll soon see the parts that need just a little explanation from you so that they make more sense to him. It is the *shared* experience, the *shared* interest and *discussion* which makes television a wonderful medium for learning (which is one of the very good reasons why schools use television).

Try to think of every programme watched with you as an opportunity to share some fun or to pick up an idea, and every programme watched without you is, at best, keeping him quiet for five minutes

It's much more fun to watch television with my Mummy and Daddy than to sit all alone. I see all the best programmes this way and understand them better, too, because Mummy and Daddy explain things to me.

(by Lisa, 6 yrs 3 mths)

and, at worst, positively harming his very impressionable mind.

Radio

Some local radio stations produce programmes for young children (contact the Educational Producer of your area, if in doubt) and the B.B.C. offers an excellent variety, such as:

1 'The Music Box' – folk songs, listening music and simple games from all over the world are presented in a lively and informal way. It is not available to Welsh listeners.
2 'Listening Corner' – songs, games and stories told by a variety of well-known storytellers. Available to English listeners only.
3 'Playtime' – a variety of movement, rhymes, songs and stories which is particularly suitable for 4 to 5 year olds. It is not available to Scottish listeners.
4 'Poetry Corner' – a collection of new poems, old favourites and traditional rhymes selected to introduce young children to the pleasure of using language in poetry and song. It is not available to Scottish listeners.
5 'Hopscotch' – games, stories, songs, poems and rhymes. This programme is for Scottish listeners only.

As with children's television programmes, there are very useful booklets

I like School. I used to play with the sand in class one and class two. When I went up in to class five I began to play football and cricket. I play monsters with my friend. I like stories on listening to hear the radio.

(by Paul, 6 yrs 9 mths)

available for the above radio programmes which cost between 40p to 85p each. You can obtain them by writing to, The School Broadcasting Council for the United Kingdom, Villiers House, The Broadway, London W5 2PA.

Why *is* the radio so important? Your child has to *concentrate* for he has no pictures to help him (as he does with television) so he is developing his *imagination* and the crucially important skill of *listening* at the same time. There is a vast difference between *hearing* and *listening* – *think* about it! Ask yourself if your child will learn anything readily at school if he can't concentrate or listen. These programmes which last about 10 minutes will help, providing you sit with him *and* join in the songs and rhymes, etc. Moreover, you can talk to him about it afterwards and find out just how carefully he has listened.

Again, it's the shared experience that's so important and you will very soon see how best to help your child if you enter into each experience with him. You can see by Paul's writing (6 yrs 9 mths) that he enjoys 'listening to hear stories on the radio' (as well as the many other activities he enjoys in school!). Teachers do not regard the radio as a medium to be dismissed just because they have the added advantages of television, videos and computers . . . nor should you!

Books and comics

If you let your child choose *suitable* comics for his age, they are useful. He is following a story by looking at a sequence of pictures. This is called 'pre-reading' and is one of many activities which will prepare him for learning to read. You'll find other suggestions elsewhere in this book. Comics, of course, also offer other useful activities, such as puzzles.

Books, however, are much more important, and, though they can be expensive, no home need be without them.

Encourage relatives and friends to buy him a book for his birthday and for Christmas, and you can make sure he has a supply of his own very special books by using the suggestions under 'home-made books' on page 20.

Get him his own ticket at the library and visit it every week: you'll find the youngest children most welcome and the librarians very helpful. Help him to choose his book, show him how to turn the pages and how to care for books. Do *you* visit the library weekly and care for books? There's nothing quite like practising what you preach! If he sees you only flicking through a magazine or reading the sports page of a newspaper he's hardly likely to think books are of any use or importance, let alone a source of pleasure. Seeing you use books for pleasure and information will demonstrate that there's some point in his learning to read. You know yourself how much easier it is to learn anything if you can see the point.

Read to your child *every* day. Make a habit of deliberately switching off the television set – you're going to have to choose your stories carefully, and tell them well, to compete with television! Choose books which are well illustrated, and discuss the pictures. Ask him to reflect and to predict – 'What *has* happened? What do you think *might* happen?' Use your common sense, though, for you'll put him off the book if you start asking questions when he's tired and all he wants is the comfort and pleasure of simply sitting on your knee to listen to a story. Your child will enjoy all the well known stories such as 'The Three Pigs', 'Goldilocks and the Three Bears', 'Little Red Riding Hood', which you enjoyed as a child. If you weren't fortunate enough to enjoy being told stories by either your mother or your father, all the more reason you should make sure *your* child doesn't miss out. You'll find this will become your favourite time of the day, as it should be for your child.

Now and again, when you are reading a story from a book, draw your child's

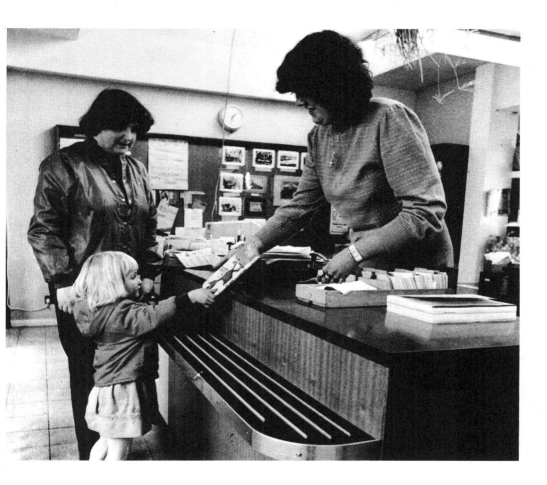

attention to the *words*, and demonstrate to him that you are reading from left to right, line by line, from the top of the page to the bottom.

Stop now and think for a moment about your own dependence on *words* during your daily life, and then think about taking every opportunity to point out at least some of these words to your child. For instance: the labels on packets and tins, sweets and toys; instructions on pedestrian crossings; titles of television programmes; the name of your house or the street where you live, and so on. He's only likely to notice the words you point out to him.

Book clubs provide a choice of paper

back books some of which have cassettes which gives your child the oppportunity to follow the story by both looking and listening. For details of the See-Saw Book Club write to Scholastic Publications Ltd., Westfield Road, Southam, Leamington Spa, Warwickshire CV33 0BR.

Recommended books

Ladybird Books Ltd. offer a wide variety and at a very competitive price. Macdonald Educational Ltd. offer a similarly wide variety but are not as cheap. They are good value, nevertheless.

Books written by:

Gareth and Jean Adamson – all the 'Topsy and Tim' books, Blackie & Son Ltd.

Jan and Stan Berenstain, such as *Inside, outside, upside down*, and the *Dr Seuss* books, Collins Sons & Co. Ltd.

Dick Bruna, Methuen Children's Books Ltd.

Eric Carle, such as *The Very Hungry Caterpillar*, Hamish Hamilton Ltd.

P.D. Eastman, such as *Big dog, little dog*, Collins Sons & Co. Ltd.

Pauline Burke, such as *The abc 123 Story Book*, Longman Group Ltd.

Pat Hutchins, Bodley Head Ltd.

Armada Lions, Collins Sons & Co. Ltd.

Helen Piers, Methuen Children's Books Ltd.

Richard Scarry – every book a gem, Hamlyn Pub. Group Ltd. and Collins Sons & Co. Ltd.

The above books are skilfully illustrated, but the illustrator *extraordinaire* is Brian Wildsmith. Any book illustrated by Brian Wildsmith is bound to be a winner. Look out for:

Birds, Mother Goose a book of nursery rhymes and songs, *Puzzles, Wild Animals, The Hare and the Tortoise* and *The North Wind and the Sun* (folk tales retold by Brian Wildsmith), Oxford University Press.

Your children's librarian at the local library will be pleased to help you further.

Home-made books and writing

Together with your children you can make books which will be his first simple reading books. Buy him a cheap pair of children's scissors (rounded, not pointed ends) and let him cut out pictures from old magazines or catalogues (don't be fussy about the outline: let him cut out the pictures to *his* satisfaction) and then let him stick them into a scrap book. Write his name on the front of the book. Discuss with your child the title for the book – it could be a collection of pictures of clothes, or people, or animals, or things he likes to eat, or things you buy at the fruit shop, or vehicles, or pressed wild flowers, or something he's particularly interested in at the time. Give him the chance to try to draw or paint the pictures, too. He'll usually be willing to try, provided you encourage him; and you should always praise his efforts even though it might not look to you like a dog, or a car, or a person, or anything very much at all! As he sticks each picture on to the page (you could make a flour and water paste for this, if you like) write just *one* word beneath. If it's a book about pets write *dog* underneath the picture, and so on. Write the word so that you leave a space and in future you could add the word 'A' or 'My'; you could finish up with, 'A dog has four legs', or 'My dog is called Pip', or 'My pet dog', such as Robert's opposite.

You've a long, long way to go before making up even a short sentence, though. By printing just *one* relevant word you are teaching your child that the shape of the word for dog differs from the shape of the word for cat, budgerigar, rabbit, hamster, fish, pony, etc.

Say the word as you write it, with him beside you. Never print in capital letters, except for the first letter of a name or sentence. Use the school print shown on pages 24–25.

He'll turn to these books over and over again because they're special, having his name on the front, *and* – very important – he's had the pleasure of making them with you. Without realising it he's also gained a great deal of experience by separating things into groups – which is fundamental to arithmetic (see page 23).

Never attempt to teach your child his A (ay) B (bee) C (see), nor the phonetic

My pet dog, Sam.   *(by Robert, 5 yrs 1 mth)*

alphabet, but if you ever need to talk about a letter, then be sure you *do* use the phonetic alphabet. These are the sounds you'll need to refer to, and you'll find them useful once he has started learning them at school:

a as in *a*pple	n as in *n*ame
b as in *b*all	o as in m*o*p
c as in *c*ap	p as in *p*oke
d as in *d*og	q say *'kw'*
e and in *e*lephant	r as in *r*un
f as in *f*eather	s as in *s*nake
g as in *g*rape	t as in *t*ail
h as in *h*op	u as in *u*p
i as in *i*gloo	v as in *v*eil
j as in *j*ail	w as in *w*in
k as in *k*ettle	x say *'ex'*
l as in *l*ip	y as in *y*awn
m as in *m*at	z as in *z*ebra

Encourage your child to draw, crayon, paint, chalk, model with plasticine – any activity which will help to develop and strengthen the muscles in his fingers, arm, hand and shoulder, all of which have to be controlled (especially the muscles in his fingers) if he is going to be able to control a pencil and begin writing. He'll need thick pencils and crayons, long thick paint brushes and jars of poster paints, and large sheets of paper.

He'll draw on anything (if you let him!) but look out for rolls of paper which are being sold cheaply, and ask at the wallpaper shop for any of their old, unwanted books. He'll happily paint a picture on newspaper, large paper bags or a cardboard box – you don't have to supply him with the best quality paper.

You could buy clay or dough (and perhaps, like the better quality paper, these would be nice for a treat) but you can make

a dough mixture at home which would serve the purpose just as well. Let him help you mix a 2lb bag of plain flour, a tablespoon of salt, and a few drops of oil, and bind all together with water. You could divide the mixture and add a few drops of different colours (bought at the chemist) to make it more interesting, to help teach him the names of colours, or just for a change. Keep the dough in polythene bags and it can be used time and time again. If he makes some models he's especially proud of, pop them onto a baking tray in the bottom of a cooling oven overnight, or simply let them dry out slowly till rock hard. Then he could paint them. You might like to let him varnish them, too, and give them

pride of place on the mantlepiece. You could write a label to put beside the model of his dog, then he's seeing the word 'dog' somewhere else besides in his book of pets.

Do you see that, by initially helping him to develop his finger and arm muscles, you've finished up doing much more? Discussing his efforts and taking a pride in them is just as important as the action itself – in many ways, *more* important, for the interest and pleasure you show will encourage him. Perhaps you could choose, with him, a place in the house – his room, the kitchen, anywhere – where you could display his models, drawings and paintings. Write his name *above* the pictures, with one word describing them beneath, as you

(by Jimmy, 4 yrs 0 mths)

did in the scrap book. The first word he'll be really interested in, will be his first name. Try writing it in very large bold print with a thick black pen, and let him write over your letters. His eye muscles, finger and arm muscles, *and* his powers of concentration will have to be *very well* developed before he's able to copy beneath your writing. His future teacher will not expect him to be

capable of 'copy-writing' until he's started school, so don't push him towards this stage. Use your common sense, always.

Number

You have already begun your work on number by sorting things into categories with your scrap books. You can continue this sorting experience throughout the day at home or when shopping. When you get home from the shops let him help you sort out the goods. There'll be things in your basket which need to go straight into the fridge, into the pantry, or into the bathroom. Food-stuffs can be sorted into large and small; packets and tins. Count the items by placing your finger or hand on each, as you count. If you've bought a dozen eggs, talk about a dozen ('What *is* a dozen?') and a half-dozen ('What *is* a half-dozen?'). Count each egg in the box. If

a b c d e
f g h i j k
l m n o p
q r s t u
v w x y z

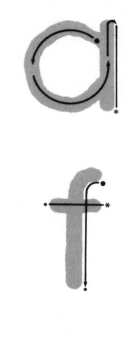

**Start at the dot, follow the arrows and
finish at the star.**

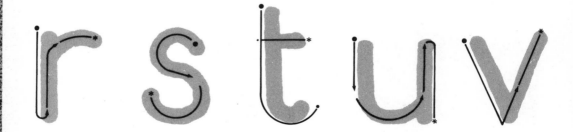

b c d e

g h i j k l

n o p q

w x y z

you're having eggs for tea ask him to get the egg-cups out so that everyone will have one egg-cup each (*don't* tell him how many). Then let him put the egg for Daddy, the egg for Mummy, the egg for himself into the egg cups. This is called 'matching' and, like 'grouping' and 'sorting', is basic to all his future understanding of arithmetic.

By letting your child help you around the house (or in the garden or at the shops . . .) you will be helping your child understand how numbers occur in life – not by doing sums (1 + 1 = 2) but by counting in different ways. Let him help you set the table and ask:

- 'How many forks have I set out?'
- 'How many knives will we need?'
- 'How many plates will we need?'
- 'Who needs a spoon for sugar?'
- 'How many don't need a spoon?'
- 'Have we enough saucers?'
- 'How many cups will we need?'
- 'Have we too many cups now?'

All the time he will be counting, matching, grouping, and sorting and it'll be fun.

Empty your handbag out every once in a while and sort the contents into things of different sizes, colours, shapes, or things that *feel* different. Young children enjoy using all their senses (i.e., touch, taste, sight, smell and hearing).

Try concentrating one day on 'sight' and empty your button box. Ask him to sort the contents into groups of large and small buttons. If you have a very large collection, reduce the number to no more than a variety of twenty buttons. After he's sorted them into two groups, ask him to guess if there are more in one group than in the other. When he's guessed, match small and large in two lines and then ask him if he thinks he was right. Count the number in each line. Notice how he answers your questions and how he is making judgements but *never* answer the questions for him. And, choose the right moment. If he is, for instance, in the middle of an absorbing game already and you interrupt it with, "**Stop** that. **Come** here – I want you to do **this** now," he'll resent the intrusion and give you very little attention. Timing is

important, as is the tone of your voice and the expression on your face, *whatever* you are doing. Enter into the spirit of the activity with enthusiasm so that he becomes as keen to play your game, as he is to play his own.

Sometime, on your own, sort out the contents of your button box, looking for groups of differing colours, shapes, textures, sizes, or buttons with one, two, three, four or more holes. Prepare yourself for the next 'button' game but also let your child sort out the contents for himself – you'll be surprised at his ability to observe differences you hadn't even thought of. The more often he plays such sorting games, the more observant he will become, of course. If you haven't a button box, or the contents seem rather limited to give him a variety of sorting experiences, take a plastic bag with you next time you visit or pass a public house. Ask for a quantity of their used bottle tops – you and your child will enjoy a surprising variety of sorting activities with these, just as you will with any oddments. It's a good idea to keep an 'oddments' box and never to throw

anything away until you've worked out how the item could be used. A 'treasure' box is also useful and might contain anything from a sea-shell, to a pebble, to an old broken necklace, to a bird's feather, etc. Let *him* decide which items should be included in his collection of 'treasures', however, for his idea of 'treasure' might not resemble yours. Sort out the contents of his box regularly. Now you know what to be on the look-out for, you'll see that the opportunities are endless – what's more it need cost you *not a single penny*.

Setting the table, sorting buttons and 'treasure', matching bottle tops, looking for things that feel similar (or different), are invaluable basic number activities. A parrot could be taught to count from 1–10, or even 1–100, but you are wasting precious time if you spend it trying to train your child to count parrot-fashion. How often, I wonder, have you observed parents urging their child to count to ten, and then sitting, with fingers crossed, hoping he's learned the correct sequence at last? He may start off very confidently with: 1, 2, 3 – pause – 5, 4, 6, 7 – longer pause – 8, 2, 6, 7, 9, 10.

Even if your child can repeat the sequence as well as next-door's parrot, I'm afraid all your efforts will have been to little real purpose; it will not have given him any understanding, and it's the *understanding* which is *vital*. You should, by the way, refer to the very first number as 0 not 1 (it is also known as 'nothing', 'naught', 'empty', 'zero'). Many young children – because they have grown up in the 'space age' – have learned to chant parrot-fashion:

'Ten, nine, eight, seven, six, five, four, three, two, one, zero, *Blast off.*'

Try questioning yours about the meaning of 'zero', however, and you'll find him looking at you blankly! He'll have a very clear idea in his mind of the meaning of 'Blast off', though!

Would you like to try another game which will deepen his understanding of what a number stands for, and which will cost nothing? It's very simple – though your child might not find it simple. Ask him to find you *one* spoon, *two* shoes, *three* crayons, *four* tins, *five* books. Give him affectionate praise when he's successful, and, if he makes a mistake, discuss this without giving him the feeling that he's failed. You can complicate the game by asking for *one red* sock, *two blue* mugs, *three yellow* dusters, *four white*

10, 9, 8, 7, 6, 5, 4, 3, 2, 1, ZERO - BLAST OFF!

handkerchiefs, *five green* apples. Do make sure, of course, that everything is safely within your child's reach. Concentrate your games on numbers from 0–5. If the objects are there, yet he cannot bring you the correct number, let alone the correct object, don't display disappointment – he has taught *you* a valuable lesson, which is that he needs much more experience. Start again and ask him to bring you his favourite toy car; if he brings half a dozen, ask him to choose *one* out of the pile, Praise him, even to excess, as he proceeds to understand the difference between 0 and 1, and 1 and 2, 1 and 3, 4 and 2, 3 and 5 – also all the differences between red and blue, rough and smooth, shiny and dull, long and short, high and low, over and under, wide and narrow, in and out, and so on. You may well be wondering what these various groups have got to do with 'number'. Your child has to learn that every object has a name and that each can be put into one or more categories. For instance, let's suppose you have on the table before you:

1 glass tumbler } common property 'glass'
2 glass ash-tray

3 pot mug } common property 'pot'
4 pot lighter

5 box of matches

There are two obvious groups here – 1 and 2, and 3 and 4, with 5 in a group on its own. You could, however, group 1 and 3 together; and 2, 4 and 5 together. Try looking for as many common – or uncommon – properties as you can. You'll soon see that one object can belong – or not belong – to a wide variety of groups. When you are playing 'grouping' games with your child, ask him if there are *more* in one group than in another – if so, how many more? Or, if there are *fewer* in one group than in another – if so, how many fewer? Put them all together again so that the total can be recounted. Don't forget to involve all his senses, and try to use your

own interest and pleasure to stimulate his learning.

In a general sense, of course, daily life gives you so many opportunities of increasing his familiarity with numbers and the *figures* which symbolise them: the number of your house; the number of the bus which takes you from home to town; your telephone number; the number 1 on a one penny piece, or the number 2 on a twopenny piece, and so on. He's only likely to notice numbers if you point them out to him.

Baking

Helping you to bake is an extremely enjoyable and valuable way for your child to learn about number, mainly because he'll be given the chance to use all his five senses at once. If you're worried about the mess, lay newspapers all around the baking table *or* polythene sheets which can be wiped clean afterwards. Perhaps one of the easiest ways to start baking with your child is to buy an 'easy cake mix' – at least you're sure of success and he'll get such satisfaction seeing everyone enjoy 'his' baking. However, there are many very reasonably priced recipe books for young children and he *is* perfectly able to make delicious sweets, savouries, biscuits, and cakes. You won't forget to count each spoonful carefully or, to count how many you've made or, if there are more than 5 or less than 5 and so on. Let him have some of the spare pastry when you're baking; he could make the jam tarts for tea – 'matching' jam to tart. Even if they resemble red concrete more than jam tarts, you will enjoy them, won't you?!

What else will your child be learning, over and above counting, when you include him in your baking sessions? He'll see you referring to a recipe book; see you working out quantities, using weights, jugs, spoons; learn the *real* meaning of lengths of time; see raw ingredients, handle them, ask what

(by Darren, 6 yrs 7 mths)

they are and where they come from; exercise his muscles in hands and arms; learn new words such as 'whisking', 'stirring', 'melting', 'blending', 'kneading', 'pouring', 'beating', 'consistency', and so on. He'll learn just as much if you let him help you with the washing up, too: push his sleeves up and wrap a waterproof apron around him; fill the sink with warm, soapy water and he'll happily do *all* the washing up while you do a dozen other jobs nearby. (It would be as well, however, to remove fragile glass articles and suchlike, for everyone's sake!) Try not to think of him being in the way, or being a nuisance, or prolonging a job you could have finished hours before – sometimes it takes you twice as long to do a job, simply because you've attempted to occupy your child and yourself in quite *separate* activities.

Darren, in his illustration above, shows us that despite all the work his mother has to do, she can still find sufficient time to include him in preparing the meal for father when he comes home from work – Darren is *part* of the family and has not been separated from it by being told to go elsewhere at the very moment when he could, in fact, not only learn a great deal, but also be extremely helpful.

Games and toys

Your child's whole life is a game! As he plays, he learns. Whether he's making a new scrap book, helping you to dust, or to bake, or to mend the car, to him it's a game. Anything new is exciting, of course, though he will want (and need) to repeat

enjoyable experiences. This gives him the practice he needs – which we all need – to make perfect. Doing something again and again, discovering new and better ways of doing things, are all a vital part of learning.

Play all the well-known card games such as 'snap', 'pairs', 'happy families', 'beg o' my neighbour', and the well-known board games such as 'snakes and ladders' (there's your chance to count – rather than to *chant* – backwards as well as forwards!). Jigsaws help to focus his attention on shape (more 'pre-reading' work), as do 'posting' boxes with a variety of shapes which your child has to match. The following is an excellent game which will help to train his memory. Let him choose five articles and place them together on a tray. Tell him to turn around while you take one away. He then has to look and recall the missing article. As he gets quicker at recalling the missing article, add to the number on the tray. He'll enjoy

the game all the more, of course, if you take it in turns to remove the article and he sees *you* looking perplexed! Do remember that whatever game you're playing, it must be for *fun* – if he starts to get the feeling that you're 'testing' him, he won't play with you any more.

Games which help him practise the skill of listening are also important: whispering and echo games; games such as 'Simon says' and 'I spy' (remember to use the phonetic alphabet, though). If you have a cassette recorder, record a variety of everyday sounds, such as the kettle boiling, running water into a sink and then the sounds of the sink being emptied, the front door bell, the vacuum cleaner, the carpet sweeper, the light switch being turned on and off, extracts of music which introduce his favourite television programmes, the sound of his own voice and those of his family and friends, and so on. The game 'sound lotto' is a useful and inexpensive way of linking sight and sound. Just as your child has to interpret what he *sees*, he has, also, to learn how to interpret what he *hears*. So often, we make the assumption that if our children can hear what is said, they understand the message.

If you are ever in any doubt as to the best games to play with your child, ask for advice from the headteacher next time you visit her at school. She is in the best position to help you, especially if she sees you often and gets to know your child.

All children, of course, love having their own toys – more often than not they seem to have more toys than they know what to do with! Try to be sure you buy some toys which will help develop the fingers such as small and large bricks; and screwing, fitting-together games.

Look at any toy very carefully before buying and ask yourself:

1 Can we afford it?

2 Does he need it?
3 Will he play with it for long or lose interest in it quickly?
4 Does it offer more than fun and, if so, what?
5 Could we make something out of 'nothing' which would serve the same purpose?
6 Is it suitable for his age?
7 Am I buying impulsively, having been attracted by colourful or elaborate packaging?
8 Is the toy safe to play with? Has it any sharp edges or corners, or has it parts which loosen too readily, for instance?
9 Is the toy durable?
10 Might it not be as well to ask for a demonstraton, or, at least to ask if a sample pack could be examined?

Remember, your child could get as much pleasure (and learn *more*) from several large cardboard cartons and a newspaper hat than from one costly toy. His vivid imagination does not need lots of extras! Watch your child one day when he's playing with his friends and you'll soon realise the important part imagination plays. Bought toys, once the novelty has worn off, very often *restrict* their games, which is why they're often discarded. Girls *and* boys love dressing-up so you'd be wise to start collecting or making articles which will help to make his imaginative play even more exciting – his 'dressing-up' box will be a constant source of pleasure both to your child and to his friends.

Making articles for his 'dressing-up' box and making toys needs just a little imagination and everyone helping – including your child on occasions. You can make jigsaws, for instance, from old birthday and Christmas cards – the larger the card the better. Stick the picture onto an old cardboard carton and cut out the very simple shapes yourselves. You could use the bottom of the carton to make up your own board game. If you get stuck for ideas, ask for help next time you're in the library or spend some time browsing round a toy shop where you'll get inspiration and *not* spend the money you can ill-afford!

Recommended Toys

Write to the following firms for their catalogues.

Globe Education,
Globe Book Services,
Brunel Road,
Basingstoke RG21 2XJ

E. J. Arnold & Son Ltd,
Butterley Street,
Leeds LS10 1AX

Early Learning Centre,
11 Crown Steet,
Reading RG1 2TQ

Hestair Hope Ltd,
St Philip's Drive,
Royton,
Oldham OL2 6AG

Philip & Tacey Ltd,
North Way,
Andover,
Hampshire SP10 5BA

'Four to Eight',
Medway House,
Faircharm Industrial Estate,
Evelyn Drive,
Leicester LE3 2BU

Galt Early Stages,
Brookfield Road,
Cheadle,
Cheshire

E.S.A. Vital Years,
Fairview Road,
Stevenage,
Herts.

'Community Playthings',
Robertsbridge,
E. Sussex TN32 5DR

(N.B.: Catalogues sent post free.)

One of the advantages in browsing through the catalogues is that they're categorised and state the age group for which the toy is intended. For example, E.S.A. has several pages of first toys, early learning, etc., which are subdivided into language, mathematics, etc. Most of the catalogues will help you understand better the purpose of the toy. An additional advantage in sending for these catalogues is that once they've served *your* purpose, the pictures can be cut out and used for the home-made books you make with your child. He'll find the pictures fascinating, and they'll be an invaluable basis for conversation.

Also make enquiries, either at your library or at the nearest Citizens Advice Bureau, for the nearest 'Sheltered Workshop'. There is a variety of 'Workshops', e.g. for the blind, the mentally handicapped and jobless, and they produce an excellent variety of toys. Moreover, they will make toys to your specification.

The following is a short list of suitable toys for the two to five year-old (I've not included large toys such as prams, tricycles, slides, etc.)

1 A variety of large and small building bricks;
2 Hammer and peg toys;
3 Posting boxes;
4 Construction kits;
5 Jigsaws;
6 Discovery balls, musical balls, finger balls;
7 A variety of card games such as 'Supersnap' and 'Trapsnap';
8 Large Lego;
9 Giant dominoes and lotto systems;
10 Skittles;
11 A variety of 'Sorting Kits', such as animals, shapes, cars, buttons, etc.
12 Sticklebricks, *or* Octons, *or* Mobilo, *or* Construct-o-straws.

Music

Your child will *hear* music just about everywhere he goes, but that's not the same as *listening* to music. He can enjoy listening to your music, of course, but you should teach him his own music, that is nursery rhymes, jingles, and songs. Tap, pat, clap the rhythms and make *his* music fun!

You could buy him some musical instruments such as a toy xylophone or a tambourine, but he'll get as much musical experience and more fun from instruments you make together at home. Here are a few ideas: fill milk bottles or jam jars, or medicine bottles with varying amounts of water and tap out your tunes with a teaspoon (add different colours to the water to make the instrument more attractive – this will be yet another way to

help teach him his colours); add a handful of rice, lentals, dried peas or barley to a used washing-up liquid container, and seal the end with Sellotape (you could paint and varnish this to make it more attractive); stitch bells to a piece of elastic which will fit around your child's wrists or ankles; save the two halves of a used coconut; clean and bleach, paint and varnish, bones of various sizes obtained from the butcher. He can use those to beat out the rhythm of his favourite pieces of music, or to make up his own rhythms, or to copy a variety of rhythms which you've made up. *Make music fun* (Dryad Press) by Avril Dankworth is a useful pamphlet which will give you many more interesting musical ideas. *Sounds Fun* (Schools Council) by T. Wishart is an enjoyable book of musical games.

The world is an interesting place!

You don't need to convince your child that the world is an interesting place – his daily explorations convinced him of this long ago! Each day he'll discover something new and, given your encouragement, he'll want to explore even more. What you need to do is to look more closely at his world and see it as it surrounds him – not just from his height but considering his lack of understanding. Remember, also, that there's a great deal you take for granted just because you've been surrounded for longer by the same things. You might see your child looking closely at a daisy for the first time or listening intently to the 'tick-tock' of the clock on the mantlepiece. Grasp the opportunity to look at the daisy and the workings of the clock, with your child close beside you. Discover together and ask of yourself and of him: 'I wonder why . . .?', 'I wonder how . . .?', 'I wonder if . . .?'

If you should have a particular hobby or interest — whether it's home-decorating, wild animals, dressmaking, car maintenance, gardening, bird-watching, fishing, or stamp-collecting — try to include your child. Your interests will become his interests and you his best teacher. No one would pretend that this is an easy task: you'll need patience and you'll have to adapt *your* way of thinking to the way your *child* thinks. He cannot, for instance, think in the abstract (it will be *many* years before he's able to do this), nor can he reason as you are able to reason. In fact, he thinks

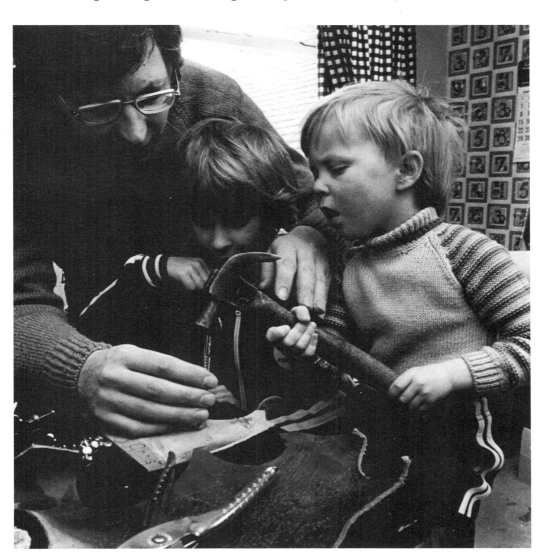

intuitively and, you'll notice, very often inconsistently. He needs explanations – through discussions – which will help to develop his powers of reasoning and he'll learn to reason, furthermore, (given years of practice) by actually *doing* and *seeing* for himself. He needs to experience everything *directly* if he's going to make *sense* of the world he lives in. Arrange outings to the nearest zoo, museums, and art galleries; he'll not be interested in everything, of course, but you can be on the look-out for those things you think might be of interest such as exhibitions organised especially for young children. If there is a railway station nearby, spend an hour or so looking around and watching the trains arrive and depart – even better, buy a cheap day excursion and let him experience what it is like to travel by train. (Many children, these days, take *flying* to foreign parts for granted as well as travelling from home to town by *car* – yet have never experienced travelling by *train* or *bus*!) It's also surprising that so many children have not even enjoyed all the amenities offered at the local park – which is almost on the door-step and costs nothing.

You'll find the world is much more exciting, wonderful, and interesting, if you look at it through your child's eyes and ears. You could also become as curious as he is, and he'll benefit from your curiosity just as he will benefit from his own.

Learning independence

Before your child starts school he should have learned to be independent of you – not, of course, in the sense that he could manage his own life without you! He does need to experience, however, what it's like not to have you around – he's going to have to come to terms with this when he starts school, so the more experience he has of being separated from you, the better he will adjust to school. He should be accustomed to mixing with adults other than those in his family, *and* with friends of his own age; nursery schools and playgroups give your child this experience (*and much more*) but if these should not be available in your area, you should start to think of ways in which you could do something by co-operating with other

mothers who are in the same position as yourself. The more shy, clinging or dependent your child is, the more effort you should make, though you should release him gradually from the absolute dependence he has on you. By the time he is four years old he should have had some experience of sleeping overnight at his grandparents' home – or an aunt's ('real' or otherwise) home, and thoroughly enjoyed the experience. Long before that, however, he'll have enjoyed going to play at his friends' homes as well as entertaining them at his home, *and* will have learned that when he's playing away from home, you aren't always there to turn to for comfort, or to take sides if there's a dispute. He'll learn that other adults can be relied upon, as well as yourself. It is regrettable that some parents would *rather* their child were entirely dependent upon them, than released and allowed to become independent.

Unfortunately some parents, rather than *insist* that their child takes some responsibility, prefer, for instance, to tidy up after him. Long before he starts school he should know how to look after his toys, his clothes, and be willing and able to tidy up or clear away. This means he's learned to accept responsibility. It's not unreasonable to expect him to do such jobs – they will certainly be expected of him when he starts school. Teachers have to spend too much time training children to do jobs which they should have learned during the years at home. It really isn't too difficult for you to train your child to act responsibly, compared with the task of a teacher attempting to teach thirty or more children *at once*. Even if you have begun the task of teaching your child to accept responsibility, there'll still be much more he has to learn, both at home and at school.

If he's to be given responsibility, then he must also be *trusted*. So do trust him to do the washing up, find the spanner, look after his patch in the garden, and so on. (Incidentally, you don't have to have a

garden to grow things – he can grow mustard and cress, flowers, plants, even tomatoes on a sunny window-sill.) He'll need guidance and help, of course, but will benefit additionally if he feels *you* have learned that *he* can be relied upon. Give him plenty of praise when he does do a job well (especially when he's just beginning to learn the meaning of responsibility), yet also make sure he understands that he is simply doing what you expect of him. Strike a happy balance, and use your common sense.

Also, *be patient*. He'll not learn how to fasten buttons, put on socks, put on his trousers or jumper, pull up zips or fasten buckles over-night: it's a *slow* process and requires lots of practice on his part (as well as patience on your part!).

There has been – and still is – a great deal of discussion about the best ways of disciplining children. There's no easy answer, for every child responds differently to different forms of punishment. Few sensible parents believe that no child should ever be punished, just as there are few who believe no child should ever be rewarded. Most parents, in fact, do believe that reward *and* punishment are necessary: the difference of opinion rests in *what* rewards and *what* punishments. You know your child (presumably) – you also know that each child in your family responds differently, and that this doesn't help matters. However, you can decide which

rules you insist must be observed, making sure these are reasonable according to his age. Your rules will have to be adjusted as your child grows older though there will be some *standards* which you might always expect adherence to, irrespective of age. Whilst you should make allowances for your child's lack of understanding, you should never feel guilty about the standards you aspire to as a family. It isn't easy to abide by the standards you set — more often than not the whole world seems to be conspiring against you — but, if you're convinced that the standards (or 'rules') are

right, then have the courage of your convictions and stick to them firmly. Your child won't resent your rules provided you stick to them and they seem to him to be reasonable and fair. (More difficulties arise with young children through rules being observed strictly one day and not at all the next, than through rules not being seen as 'fair', however.)

Support one another — as husband and wife — so that he doesn't 'play off' one against the other. Have a tactful chat with grandparents, relations, and friends who might tend to overlook some aspects of your child's behaviour which you don't want overlooked. You need all the support you can get, for the youngest of children seem to have an uncanny knack of knowing whom they can exploit to *their* best advantage.

Independence isn't easy either for you to teach *or* for your child to learn. However, it's something he's been learning from the time he first decided he wanted to feed himself (or even before). The wise parent has taught him how to handle a spoon and pusher, and spoon and fork, and knife and fork, and has not frustrated *his* desire for independence by continuing to *spoon-feed* him. Curb the desire you might have to 'spoon-feed' him in any way as he grows up and yet, at the same time, make sure he understands that learning to be independent does *not* mean going his own way (which is often at everyone else's expense!) and always doing as he pleases.

I hope these suggestions have helped you to understand that there's much you can do with your child day by day – incidentally, as well as deliberately. You may, for instance, deliberately have to think out your baking sessions and organise yourself well beforehand if he's to *learn* with any sense of *pleasure*. Most of the suggestions, however, are intended to help you be more aware of the everyday learning moments in your child's life. It doesn't take, for instance, that much more time to let him help you count each item out of your basket. If you're too busy that day to sort, group or match the items, try to make time the next day. Grasp the moments when you can, and remember that, in any case, most young children soon lose interest in any one activity so it's important that you don't force or push them beyond the point where their interest wanes, or you'll lose them and their enthusiasm. They'll return to the activity happily, another day.

thinking of school -Have I a choice

Unless you're prepared to travel, many of you will have no choice of primary school. The majority of parents usually select the school nearest to their home. However, by law you are entitled to choose which school you wish your child to attend after the age of five. At present, when more and more small schools are being closed or being amalgamated with other schools, it's likely that you'll want to visit those that are accessible and find out how they function. This applies also to parents who move from one area to another and who know nothing about the schools nearby. You can begin by asking other parents for their opinion but be prepared for conflicting reports. It is, in any case, necessary that you talk to the headteachers of those schools in which you're interested. Phone the school, explain your position to the headteacher and ask for an appointment.

All headteachers' time is precious, so don't expect them to spend more time with you than they can afford. You'll be given as much time as is possible and an opportunity to return. To save time you might be given a prospectus or an information sheet (which answers many of the questions below) and this you can browse over at home. Perhaps, therefore, you should ask first of all if the school has a prospectus.

The following questions are examples of those put to me by parents and I've been impressed by those who not only come well prepared with relevant queries but who also briefly record my replies in a note-book — obviously this is a sensible idea if they're not to go home uncertain and confused. The meetings are informal and several cups of coffee or tea are consumed . . . providing I've got time!

Invariably the first questions I'm asked concern *organisation* — and therefore we proceed thus:

  ✓1 'Do you group the children according to age or by some other means?'
    2 'Why? What are the advantages and

are there any disadvantages?'

3 'Would you describe your school as "progressive" or "traditional"?'

4 'How many teachers are on the staff and how experienced are they?'

5 'How many children are there in each class?'

6 'Do the children remain with one teacher for a year? Are there any specialist teachers? Is there any team-teaching?'

7 'Which reading schemes do you use?

8 'Do you do modern maths? Do the children know the multiplication tables off by heart before they go to the junior school?'

9 'Do the teachers set home-work?'

10 'How do you record the children's progress and are these records secret?'

11 'Do you test the children? Are the results secret?'

12 'Is this school well equipped?'

13 'Have the staffs of the nursery, infants' and junior schools agreed standards?

What provision do you make to ensure the children transfer happily from one department to another?'

14 'What are the school rules? How are children punished?'

$$8 \times 76 = 608, \ldots$$
$$9 \times 76 = 684 \ldots$$
$$10 \times 76 = 760 \ldots$$
$$11 \times 76 = 836 \ldots$$

15 'Is there a P.T.A. or Parents' Association? If not, why not?'

16 'How often do parents and teachers meet?'

17 'Is there a school fund? How is money raised and how is it used?'

18 'Is there a parent representative on the Governing Body?'

19 'Is the building in good repair?'

20 'Are school meals cooked on the premises?'

21 'Can the children bring a packed lunch?'

22 'Is there a separate dining hall?'

23 'Who supervises the children during the lunch hour?'

24 'What happens if a child is ill or has a serious accident at school?'

25 'Can I visit the school at any time or do I always have to make an appointment?'

Having supplied the parents with an answer to their queries and given them further information which is applicable to my school, I then escort them around the school. They visit the classrooms, are introduced to the teaching *and* non-teaching staff, and are shown anything which I think might be of interest. When you are touring the school you should bear the following in mind:

1 Do the children appear relaxed and happy, yet well-controlled? Are they friendly and courteous and working purposefully?

2 Do the teachers appear happy? Are they friendly and courteous and prepared to answer your questions?

3 Does the headteacher appear to be on good terms with staff and children? Do the children approach her readily? Does she know their names?

4 Do you form the impression that this is a happy, well-run school?

5 Is the building clean and well cared for?

6 Do the displays in the classrooms and throughout the rest of the school strike you as being not only colourful but also interesting and relevant to the interests of young children?

7 Does the school appear well equipped?

8 Do you think your child would be well educated at this school and fit in happily?

You may be fortunate enough to be able to visit and compare two, three or more schools. What you must take into account is the fact that whilst there will be similarities between the schools there will also be many differences. Each school is likely to impress you in one way or another: perhaps you liked the look of the school; perhaps you liked the atmosphere; perhaps you took an immediate liking to the headteacher and were impressed by the staff; perhaps the displays in one school were particularly outstanding, and so on. Choosing a school *isn't* easy. In the end, you must carefully consider the notes you made when you visited the schools, weigh up all the advantages and disadvantages. re-visit if necessary, and in the last resort trust to your instinct.

thinking of school
- the next stage

Registering your child

Whether you have visited the infants' school in order to select your child's future school or simply to discover what provision is made in the only school available, there comes a time when you must register your child.

When you register your child you might find it a little formal but only because the headteacher will need to ask you many questions. If you're not asked the questions then, at least you can be prepared for them at some time: your child's full name, his date of birth (dig out his birth certificate in case that's needed too), your address, how many children you have, whether you work or not, your first names, whether you have any objections to your child being taught the Christian religion, your doctor's name, whether your child has enjoyed good health since he was born and whether you had a normal pregnancy and birth, whether he's been able to obtain a place in a nursery or playgroup, whether you are on the 'phone – and if not who can be contacted in an emergency. The headteacher may also ask if you, and the father, have employment. *You* can help *her* so much by thinking of her as a future friend who has a genuine interest in you and your child. Trust her judgement and understand that she must make these enquiries if she's to be in the best position to do her job well, In between asking questions, she'll be trying her best to put your child at ease and, inevitably, will be forming an impression of him. If he's not usually as shy as he may be at this meeting, let her know and if he *is* shy normally, let her know.

There's just one more thing you should be frank about. Tell her if you are separated and bringing up your family alone; if you are divorced and bringing up your family alone; or if you have remarried; or if you are living with someone who is in every sense (except legally) your husband or wife.

Firstly, she will *not* think any less of you and, in fact, will appreciate that you have been/are experiencing some of the same kinds of difficulties which widows and widowers go through. Secondly, this information is confidential; and, thirdly, she is in the best position to see how she might be of help to you, to your family as a whole, and *especially* to your child. She certainly won't think any the less of him *or* single him out in any way. She will quite simply be given the opportunity to approach him more *sensitively*. Knowing you are a widow or widower, for instance, she'd be careful not to say to your child (in the course of a normal conversation) ''. . . and when does your Daddy come home from work?'' or, ''. . . did Mummy knit that lovely cardigan for you?'' Neither would she approach your child (just because the circumstances are different) without care. If you are unfortunate enough to be struggling to bring up a child or a family on your own, then you could well find your child's future headteacher one of your best allies.

Visits with your child

After your child has been registered, confirm that you may call regularly with him. Visit during the morning and afternoon sessions so that your child sees a variety of activities – including playtimes. These short visits, with you, of five or ten minutes each, are invaluable. Your child will be much less anxious about starting school if he is familiar with the building and the people in it, beforehand. Ask if you can show him where the toilets are and where he'll hang his coat. Make sure he sees the staff as not only his friends, but also as your friends. A mutual consideration and respect between parents and teachers is vital not only before your child starts school but for as long as your child is at school. After each visit, talk about what you have seen and discuss your plans for the next one.

How to get there

1 Find a safe place away from parked cars.

2 Stop and wait near the kerb

3 Look all round and listen.

4 Wait for traffic to pass.

5 If no traffic near, walk straight across.

6 Keep looking and listening.

Make sure your child knows his way to and from school. Can he cope with the roads? Do *you* know the Green Cross Code? If not, get in touch with your local Road Safety Officer, whom you will find at your Council Office, and ask for a copy of *Ready for the Roads*. It's free and very informative. Even if you do intend to bring him and call for him, there might be an occasion when you are delayed. Explain to him exactly what he must do if you are not there to meet him – he either waits till you arrive or begins the journey alone. Does he know that he must *never* talk to strangers – men *or* women? Your child is too young to understand the dangers fully, but you can explain the difference between those he knows and those he doesn't know – also warn him not to accept sweets or a lift from strangers.

Other children starting school

Find out which children will be starting school at the same time as your child. Your headteacher will be able to help you here.

Get together with these parents. Be the first to open your home to them and their children so that they can play together and become friends. How much nicer to start school with a group of friends than to start knowing nobody!

My mummy and all my friends' mummies have become friends. I've been invited to play at their homes and I've invited them to our house, too. We've had parties and picnics and enjoyed all sorts of games together. I'll not be lonely when I start school, that's for sure. I don't think mummy will miss me too much, as she's made so many friends through me.

by Annmarie, 5 yrs 9 mths)

Can your child . . .?

When your child does start school he should be able to do the following:

1 Dress and undress himself

2 Remove his coat, gloves and hat and hang each item up

3 Tie his own shoelaces

4 Use the toilet properly *and* flush the toilet after use

5 Wash and dry his face and hands

6 Use a knife and fork

7 Tidy/clear away his toys

8 Use a handkerchief efficiently

9 Share his toys and be prepared to 'take turns'

10 Act confidently and responsibly

School is about to begin

The night before the first day

Let him help you get his clothes ready for the next day. Few infants' schools these days have uniforms (enquire about this, though) and there is no need to go to a great deal of expense, but even one new item will help to make his next big day rather more special. Perhaps kindly grandparents or an aunt could buy him his first school bag which will help him to feel very grown up. Pop a new colouring book and some crayons inside with a few spare tissue handkerchiefs – that will be something of his own to turn to during the first day.

Try to keep him calm and relaxed and keep to your usual routine – a warm bath and early to bed! He will probably spend most of the evening and part of the night asking if it's time to get ready for school yet! Try to understand that your child is experiencing a great mixture of emotions . . . excitement that his special day is nearly here, apprehension despite all your careful planning and reassurances, and perhaps the wish that he could stay at home with you.

All you really need is patience and common sense.

The very first morning

The day you've all been waiting for is here at last! For your child this is probably the biggest step he will ever take. He'll find a tremendous difference between home and school – even if he's been lucky enough to go part-time to a playgroup or nursery. If you haven't been sitting up with him from half past four in the morning (!) get him up in good time. Be your usual self and stick to your usual routine. Try to make sure he eats his usual breakfast before setting off on the journey. If possible, try to make it a family occasion but if Mum or Dad can't get time

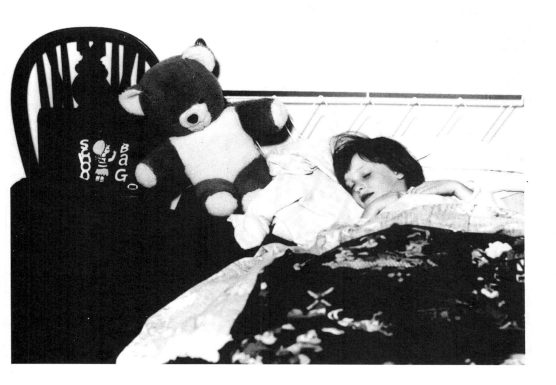

off work do make sure he's accompanied by a close relative or friend who realises the importance of this, his first day. Whether you're accompanying him or not, it's a good idea for you to arrange to meet those parents and children who are also setting out for school for the first time.

at school

Settling in

Don't worry if, after all the trouble you've taken to prepare your child for school, he howls and cries like a two-year-old on the first day! In fact, some children settle immediately and never cry; some cry on the first day and never again; some during the first week, and some, weeks later – having apparently settled down well at the beginning. You should know by now – as teachers do – that children are unpredictable! The teachers know it isn't easy to leave your child when he's sobbing and pleading with you not to leave him – but you'll have to, sooner or later. On the first day you are likely to be given ample time to choose a seat and a toy so that there isn't an immediate wrench, and the teacher will do her best to make sure he sits beside someone he knows. With luck, she'll be familiar to him through all his visits to school with you, but if she happens to be new to the school, then you must rely on her understanding and the fact that at least he knows the headteacher, the building, and a few friends. And, of course, you've been teaching him all about independence, haven't you? Should he cry, however, after you've given him time *you* must stay calm, though you will probably be feeling *just* as upset as he. Tell him you'll be back at dinner time and then *go*. If you leave the classroom with his yells ringing in your ears and your own heart bursting, look for the headteacher and ask if you can wait somewhere nearby but out of sight – you'll be astonished how soon the crying ceases and you'll go home reassured. Do remember that the teachers are used to dealing with children in this situation and can settle, comfort, and distract your child far better without you there.

Difficulties in settling in

There are, however, occasions when,

52

despite the expertise of the teacher and the most careful parental preparation, some children do not settle happily. The following are some examples of *extreme* behaviour (children react in such a variety ways):

1 Sobbing *uncontrollably and ceaselessly*, refusing to be comforted or distracted;
2 Putting up a *violent* struggle against those keeping him 'captive', resorting to kicking, biting, punching, scratching, spitting, and attempting to run home at every opportunity;
3 *Withdrawing* into a corner or somewhere out of sight, refusing to respond and preferring to be ignored.

Any child might resort to such ways of behaving for *short* periods at first – most, however, respond to the teacher's efforts to console and to distract. Reasons for protracted behaviour of this kind are not usually difficult to discover and can often be traced to something that has happened at home which you probably thought had been dealt with perfectly adequately at the time – for instance:

1 A recent move of house;
2 A new baby brother or sister arriving on the family scene;
3 Father's work suddenly taking him away from home and for long periods;
4 The death of a dearly loved grandparent;
5 Mother having to go into hospital.

Any one of these incidents might have upset him at the very time when you were doing your best to give him stability and security at home, knowing these would stand him in good stead on starting school. If – having given him time to adjust – your child seems to be *unusually* upset on starting school, think about the possible reason or reasons and then discuss these with the headteacher. She and your child's class teacher will not only be in a better position to understand why he is so extremely distressed, but also able to help you to help him. You should, in fact, alert the headteacher to any unusual circumstances at home which may significantly affect your child's behaviour at school at any time in the future. Assisting the teachers in this way gives them the chance to understand more fully your child's difficulties and to make allowances for him.

Children's fears

A few children may have understandable reservations about some aspects of school life even though, for the most part, they have settled down well. For instance, they may dread going to the toilets alone, or playing in the playground. Given time, these will become routine though it

sometimes takes a child a long time to really *enjoy* playtimes. The playground itself can hold certain fears for the new entrant:

1 The extensive area;
2 Having to share this space with more than 100 or 200 other children – the majority being older and bigger than himself;
3 The noise of so many children 'let loose' to play at once and the boisterousness of some of the older boys especially;
4 The teacher on duty probably not being *his* teacher.

Schools vary in their ways of dealing with a child's fear of the playground: his teacher might spend the first week in the playground so that he isn't suddenly left with an adult he hardly knows; or the new entrants might have a separate playtime from the rest of the school for a while; or he might be allowed to watch the other children at play from a safe vantage point; or an older brother or sister or friend might collect him from his class and take him to the playground; or he might be taken straight to the teacher on duty so that she can hold his hand and talk to him. Whatever arrangements are made, you can be sure every teacher throughout the school will be talking to her class about the younger children's fears so that the older children behave as considerately and kindly as possible. There'll also be many children in the top class who'll be only too delighted to help "keep an eye on the little ones" (*see Tracey's written work on page 63*).

Regressive behaviour

It could be that for all kinds of reasons your child takes one or two backward steps after starting school. He might begin to suck his thumb again (something he grew out of long ago) or, want the light kept on in his bedroom a little longer or, cling to you and not let you out of his sight when he is at home or, throw a few tantrums or even wet the bed. These are all signs that he's missing home and isn't yet secure at school. Let his teacher know if any signs occur (which may not be apparent at school) and she'll go out of her way to help him. You can help by giving extra affection and reassurance at home . . . and *do* be patient. He can't help these unpleasant feelings of insecurity (and he can't quite find the words which express his feelings) but he will learn to cope, with your help and that of the school.

Helping your child to cope

Starting school can be an exhausting

business – emotionally, physically, socially and mentally. Don't be surprised, therefore, if he comes home feeling very tired – give him his meal, his bath, and a cuddle and story, before getting him off to bed early.

The old (adapted) saying holds true *all* your child's life:

'Early to bed, early to rise
Makes your child healthy, wealthy, and wise'.

No one can guarantee wealth, but his teacher *can* guarantee your child will be all the healthier and all the more able to do the work she expects of him, if he's had *plenty* of sleep.

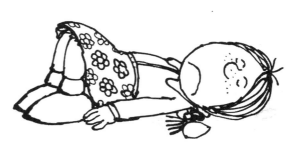

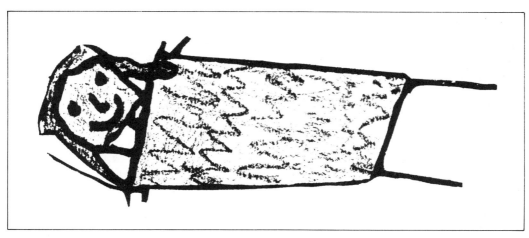

I'm dead beat and I'll soon be fast asleep

(by Lindsay, 5 yrs 5 mths)

Dinners

It is better to let your child go home for dinner for the first few weeks at least. This is probably the first time he has been away from you for any length of time, and a whole day will seem a very long time indeed. In fact, to begin with, he'll probably have no sooner got his coat and hat off at 9.00 am. than he'll be asking his teacher if it's time to go home for dinner! She can break the morning up into small units of time . . . 'after playtime', then, 'after you've painted a picture to take home', then, finally, 'after we've had a story *then* it will be time for dinner'. (Remember, she's probably having to say this, off and on,

almost all morning to most of the other new boys and girls, as well!) It's very difficult for a young child to cope with a whole day's time-table and, in any case, how lovely for him to have a *real* break at home and to see you again. It is also more difficult to eat with a large number of other children in the dining hall – everything is so much noisier, and there's so much more hurry and bustle than at home. If he should have to stay at school for dinner for any reason then be sure he knows he's going to be away from home all day and prepare him for the differences between eating at home and eating at school. All schools expect even the youngest children to remember their table manners – words like 'please' and 'thank you' haven't gone out of fashion in *or* out of the dining hall.

Taking an interest

Don't be surprised if your child comes home day after day reluctant to tell you what he's been doing all day! You'll probably get the same answer as all the other parents, such as 'nothing much', or 'just playing'. Ask, but don't pester him. You'll get news as soon as he's good and ready to give it – freely! When that happens, show a keen interest and ask him a few questions – he'll be disappointed if you *don't* appear interested at the very time when he's got some news to pass on to you. He may come home one day with a long involved story which you can scarcely make sense of, but which, nevertheless alarms you, such as that he was set upon by the whole school at playtime. Try to take most of his tales with a pinch of salt unless, of course, you're really alarmed, in which case visit school and find out what has actually happened. The headteacher will make enquiries for you. If there was an incident of some kind, it's more than likely she has already dealt with it. You must allow her, by the way, to make the decision about punishments, for she has to consider a variety of factors. She is in a unique position of responsibility for the school community as a whole, and can therefore be relied upon to be as fair as possible.

Clothing

Uniform or no uniform, do make sure his clothes are as comfortable, practical, and manageable as possible. The overwhelming majority of headteachers do welcome variety of dress so you shouldn't have the problem of trying to make a uniform comfortable! If your child is having difficulty in learning to tie his laces, then buy slip-on shoes for school. You cannot imagine how much time a teacher wastes in

tying laces, fastening buttons and buckles, pulling on socks and tights, pulling up zips and so on, for thirty or more children, especially after P.E. (Physical Education) lessons. That's one very good reason why the clothes he wears should be manageable. Name all articles of clothing which could be mistaken for another child's, such as anoraks, duffle coats, wellingtons and boots. Some children become very distressed when they can't find their own coat or boots, and it is another time-consuming job for the teacher, trying to sort one out from all the others. A good tip: give your child his own clothes peg to clip his wellingtons or boots together. It only takes one child to slip and send thirty pairs of boots flying in all directions!

Possessions

If your child should come home with another child's toy in his pocket or a toy belonging to school *don't* imagine he's started a rather early career in thieving! He's taken a momentary fancy for it and really does not understand 'stealing' as we understand it. Simply explain calmly and clearly that the toy isn't his and make *him* give it back to the child or to his teacher. You have no need to feel ashamed, and it makes matters worse if you try to hide the fact that it has happened. You'd be surprised at the number of times a day a teacher has to stop everything and play 'hunt the thimble' for a toy, which has mysteriously vanished into somebody's pocket! It is part of her job to teach your child to respect other people's property, to care about people other than himself, to ensure that he learns to behave in a controlled way, and to learn the difference between 'right' and 'wrong'. Young children are *essentially* and *only* interested in themselves, and learning to consider others, for instance, is a long, slow process which takes years of experience and guidance. Any moral training at school pre-supposes a foundation established by you at home. The school will support the child's basic moral awareness and extend it to fit the much larger social setting of the classroom and the school, but at *every* stage in the life of the schoolchild, the

home influence is *crucial* in determining whether or not he is going to grow up to be a responsible, thoughtful adult.

Should your child lose anything at school (it will probably be genuinely mislaid, *not* stolen), let the teacher or the headteacher know as soon as possible. Everyone, including the caretaker and cleaners, if necessary, will be alerted to make a search so that the item can be found.

Punctuality and attendance

Please make every effort to see that your child not only attends school regularly but also arrives *punctually*. Such good habits, begun now, will serve him well not just for the rest of his school days but in later life too. If he is absent and likely to have to stay at home for more than two or three days, let the headteacher know by sending a note, or telephoning, or calling. You should make sure to keep her well-informed if your child suffers from an actute illness or has to be admitted to hospital for any reason.

Illness

If your child is unwell and under treatment from the doctor, you'd be wise to keep him at home until the treatment has been completed. Do *not* send him to school with medicine. No member of staff can reasonably take the responsiblity for giving out medicines during the day – remember, it *is* a school, not a clinic or a hospital. The only exceptions any headteacher is likely to make to this rule are for those children requiring *essential* daily medication – such

as phenobarbitone. If your child suffers from a serious long-term illness such as epilepsy or diabetes, the headteacher should be made fully aware of the fact before your child starts school, *and* kept informed about the results of hospital visits so long as he is at school.

Comparing your child

Try – please try – *not* to compare your child with another. Your child is unique. He *looks* different, *learns* differently, *reacts* differently, and is always *himself*. Hearing you say to another parent, 'I wish my child could write as well/read as well/paint me a picture which *looks* like something/tie his laces/mix with other children better/keep himself clean/blow his nose . . .' is hurtful, damages his self-confidence and self-respect, and makes him feel unloved. He needs to know you love him and respect him, so do admire what he *can* do well. If you are worried about his lack of progress at school then find out from his teacher if you *need* to be worried and ask for ways of helping and encouraging him but not within your child's hearing. Discuss your worries together, as parents, but, again, not in front of your child.

Remember that the child with over-anxious parents is always at a disadvantage, for he'll become as anxious as yourselves and will feel as if he's never likely to please you, and there lies disaster. However, the child with interested, caring parents who show pleasure in his every effort will be well rewarded for he will grow in confidence *and* learn successfully. Learning in any case, comes in fits and starts – there'll be times when he seems to learn quickly and readily, other times when he will seem to be 'taking a breather'. It's rather like his physical growth – he'll suddenly seem to be growing taller, and then have a period when he stops growing in height and begins to 'fill out'.

Criticisms of the school

If you're critical of the school, the headteacher, or the teacher on any occasion, you'd be wise to discuss this between yourselves but *not* in front of your child. No teacher would think of saying in front of your child: '. . . mind you, he's got an untidy/strange/peculiar/incapable set of parents'. She knows how much your child loves you, and hearing her say this of you would be very hurtful to him. Similarly, he does grow fond of his teacher and forms an attachment to his school, and hearing your criticism pulls him in two directions. Should he be loyal to his teacher or believe you? It won't help his teacher, either, for he'll not learn successfully unless he has every confidence in her. Of course, if you do seriously think the teacher is failing your child, then by all means visit the headteacher and discuss the problem with her. If you're still not satisfied, and have the evidence you need, then ask the name of the Chairman of the Board of Governors and see him or her. Such cases, though, are *extremely* rare and most little niggles – and

this is usually all they are – can be very quickly sorted out by visiting the school. Go when you're calm and composed so that you can let the headteacher know everything, as you see it, quite clearly.

Trust the staff

Feel confident that, in fact, you *can* trust the staff at your child's school. Believe in their ability to teach your child according to his needs at all times. Every teacher is aware of the trust you place in him or her, and cares about your child, even though he may be one of thirty or more in a class. It is *their* job to see that *your* child gets the teaching *he* needs.

A few home-truths

These days, perhaps the most precious commodity you can give your child is your *time*. This cannot be easy if you've a large family; or if you're a one-parent family; or if mum is working, but it is vital.

It might help you to remember that the child who gets most from home gets most from school; and that the child who gets least from home gets least from school. Though a teacher will do her utmost to try to help the child who has not been helped at home, she is faced with an incredibly difficult – and, in too many cases, impossible – task.

- It won't be her fault if that child does not succeed at school.
- It won't be the child's fault if he doesn't succeed or enjoy school.
- The fault is entirely that of the child's parents.

However, if *you* have done all you can to prepare your child for school and continue to give him your love, time, interest, and support – then you can be certain he is in the best possible position to use all his unique abilities.

The last word (by the children)

Though this book is about children, for parents, I'd like to give the children the very last word.

When I Started School I began to cry and then I got used to it. I nearly played all day in class 2. It Was a nice Class. class 2. My mammy Was Very cross With me. My mammy nearly cryed because I Was being Silly. After that I Was happy at School.

What I remember about starting school   *(by Rachel, 6 yrs 11 mths)*

I like to do P.E and the television and the Xmase party and I like to bake cakeS and my Work. I like to do Writing and draw and Play a game ih the Play ground. I like to eat my Dinner. I liked Class 2 and class 4 and class 5. I Waht read books. I like to Listin to the Story. I Like to keep an eye On the Little Ones.

What I enjoy most about school   *(by Tracey, 6 yrs 11 mths)*

When I Started School I likedit and I was only 5 and I liked to work best of all and we played with plastercine. I like to play with the other children at play time. Some times I played chasy with Michelle and I was always happy and I never cried for my mammy. at School. I like to play games at school. mother day cards. I like makeing a lovely mothers day card. and I like Playing with toys.

I've always enjoyed school

(by Kerry Ann, 6 yrs 9 mt.)